About the Author

Paul Watson is a technology enthusiast and has massive experience in various technologies like web application development, automation testing, build automation, continuous integration and deployment technologies. He has worked on most of the technology stacks.
He has hands on experience on UFT, LeanFT, Selenium and Appium. He has used testing frameworks like JUnit, TestNG, Cucumber with Selenium. He has also worked on Struts, Spring, Bootstratp, Angular JS.

His hobbies include travelling to new tourist places, watching basketball, cricket and learning latest technological stuff.

A special note of Thanks to My Wife

I would like to dedicate this book to my lovely wife for loving me so much and helping me write this book. Without her support, this book would not have been a reality.

Who this book is for

This book is for automation engineers who want to learn LeanFT to automate the web and windows applications in Java.

It is assumed that reader has basic programming skills in Java language. Whether you are a beginner or an experienced developer, this book will help you master the skills on LeanFT.

The book starts with introduction of LeanFT and then dives into key concepts as mentioned below.

Supported applications,Installation ,LeanFT settings,Core Concepts,New LeanFT project in IntelliJ IDEA ,LeanFT Project in Eclipse,Object Identification and Management ,Automating Web applications, Automating windows applications,Synchronization,Assertions and Reports, LeanFT Frameworks,Converting the UFT Object Repository to Application models in LeanFT,Integrating the LeanFT tests with CI servers like Bamboo, Jenkins and TeamCity, Challenges and Solutions,LeanFT common issues and solutions,Comparing LeanFT with other tools,LeanFT Java References.

Table of Contents

1. Introduction

LeanFT stands for Lean Functional testing. This is a tool developed by HP and very similar to the Ranorex.

Key points to note about LeanFT are given below.

1. It's a licensed tool.
2. Developed by HP in 2015.
3. It's light version of UFT (QTP).
4. With LeanFT, you can write tests in .Net language as well as Java.
5. LeanFT plugin are available for Visual Studio and Eclipse.
6. LeanFT uses description programming as well as Application models to identify the objects.

2. Supported applications

LeanFT supports below types of applications.

1. Web applications on IE, Chrome, Firefox, Microsoft Edge
2. Windows application - WPF, Silverlight and more
3. SAP applications
4. Java applications
5. Standard windows and forms

In fact, all applications supported by UFT (QTP) are also supported by LeanFT.

3. Installation

3.1 Installation of LeanFT and plugins for IDEs

First visit https://saas.hpe.com/en-us/software/leanft and download the trail version of LeanFT.

Before starting the installation process of LeanFT, ensure below things

1. You have a node.js and IDE tools (Visual Studio, IntelliJ IDEA, Eclipse) already installed on your system.
2. Anti-virus software is disabled

At the time of installation, you will choose which plugins to be installed.

By default, LeanFT is installed at C:\Program Files (x86)\HP\LeanFT

Once installed, start the LeanFT engine (from installation directory or from Start menu of Windows). By default, LeanFT service runs on port 5095

Below screen shot shows the installation options during installation process. Please select full installation with visual studio and Eclipse options checked.

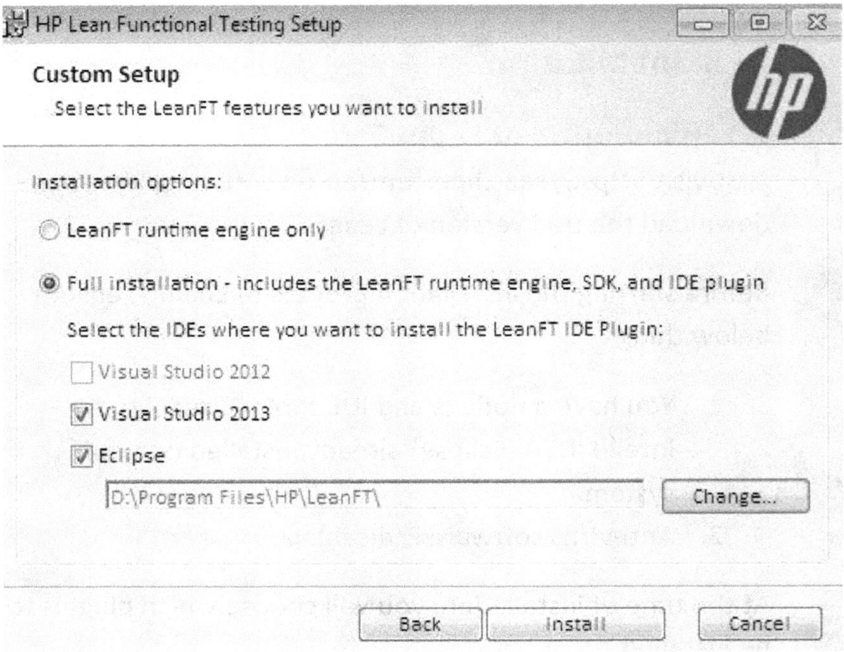

HP Lean Functional Testing Setup

Custom Setup
Select the LeanFT features you want to install

hp

Installation options:

○ LeanFT runtime engine only

◉ Full installation - includes the LeanFT runtime engine, SDK, and IDE plugin

Select the IDEs where you want to install the LeanFT IDE Plugin:

☐ Visual Studio 2012

☑ Visual Studio 2013

☑ Eclipse

D:\Program Files\HP\LeanFT\   Change...

Back   Install   Cancel

If you have got IntelliJ installed on your system, you will see below screen. Just select the checkbox next to IntelliJ IDEA to install the LeanFT plugin for IntelliJ IDEA.

LeanFT plugins

After installation of LeanFT, start the runtime engine as shown in below image. By default, engine runs on the port 5095.

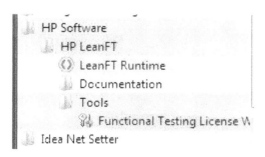

3.2 Installing browser Extensions

After installation of LeanFT, you can view the browser extension files at below location in LeanFT installation directory.

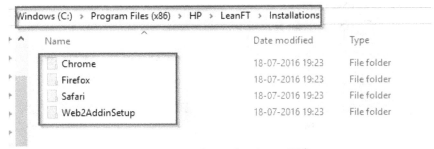

Windows (C:) › Program Files (x86) › HP › LeanFT › Installations

Name	Date modified	Type
Chrome	18-07-2016 19:23	File folder
Firefox	18-07-2016 19:23	File folder
Safari	18-07-2016 19:23	File folder
Web2AddinSetup	18-07-2016 19:23	File folder

Browser extensions for LeanFT

Just drag and drop the extension files on the browsers. Browser will install these extensions when you drop these extension files on it.

Without installing and enabling these extensions in browsers, you will not be able to automate the web application.

Below image shows the LeanFT extension enabled in chrome browser.

Extensions

Developer

Google Slides   0.9

Create and edit presentations

Details

Allow in incognito

Enabled

HP Functional Testing Agent   12.53.2027.0

Test Web Applications Using Google Chrome

Details   Options

Enabled

Allow in incognito   Allow access to file URLs

LeanFT extension in Chrome

4. Getting Started

4.1 LeanFT settings

You can view and edit the LeanFT settings from within IntelliJ IDEA IDE as shown in below image.

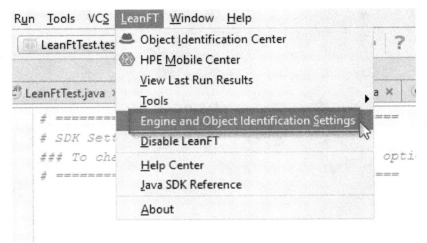

LeanFT Engine and Object Identification Settings

⟨⟩ LeanFT Settings

Engine   Object Identification

Add-ins

Select the add-ins to load

☑ Web

☑ Mobile   Show settings

☑ WPF

☑ WinForms

☐ SAPUI5

☐ SAPGUI

☑ Java

Add-ins in LeanFT

14

Engine Connection

Port	Engine idle timeout (in minutes)
5095	240

Runtime settings

Object synchronization timeout (in seconds)

20

☐ Allow LeanFT to run tests on a disconnected RDP computer

User name   Password

•••••••••••••••••••••••

Engine connection and object synchronization timeout in LeanFT

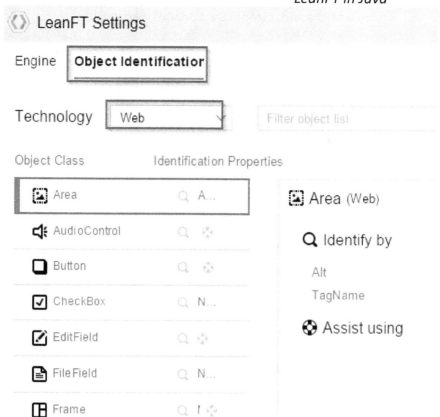

Object Identification settings in LeanFT

Here are the most important LeanFT settings.

1. Add-ins - In this section, we can specify which add-ins you want to load.
2. Engine connection and Run-time settings - In this section, we can specify the port of engine and Engine Idle time out. We can also specify object synchronization timeout. LeanFT will wait for this much time before throwing the exception.
3. Mobile Settings - In this setting we can specify the mobile center server address to automate the mobile applications with LeanFT.
4. Object Identification settings - In this tab, we can specify which properties should be used to identify the objects.

4.2 License types in LeanFT

LeanFT comes with 4 types of licenses as shown in below image.

1. Seat License - Tied to one machine
2. Concurrent license - Multiple machines can use this license
3. Commuter license
4. Remote commuter license

Functional Testing License Wizard ⓘ   ✕

SELECT LICENSE TYPE

Seat license
Install a personal license for this machine

⊘ Active License
Until 13-10-2015

Concurrent license
Install a session-based license from the license server

Commuter license
Obtain/install commuter licenses for this machine

Remote commuter license
Request and install commuter licenses for this machine when you do not have access to the license server

5. Core Concepts

5.1 Object identification Center

Object Identification Center is just like Object Spy in QTP/UFT

Object Identification Center runs in 2 modes.

1. simple - allows you to just view the object property - values
2. edit - allows you to view and edit the object property values

Object identification center allows you to do below things

1. Inspect the objects.
2. Learn about the object parent details, hierarchy.
3. Learn about the object properties and values.
4. One cool feature of Object Identification center is that generation of code snippets in Java or C#
5. Highlight the object
6. We can also capture the screenshot of the object
7. It also allows you to add the object to Application model

You can launch the Object Identification center from IntelliJ IDEA as shown in below image.

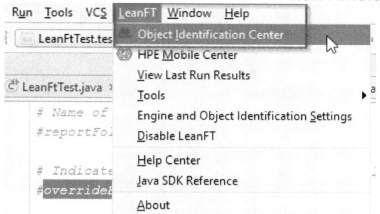

Launching LeanFT Object Identification Center in IntelliJ
IDEA

Below image shows how to inspect the elements inside web page using Object Identification Center.

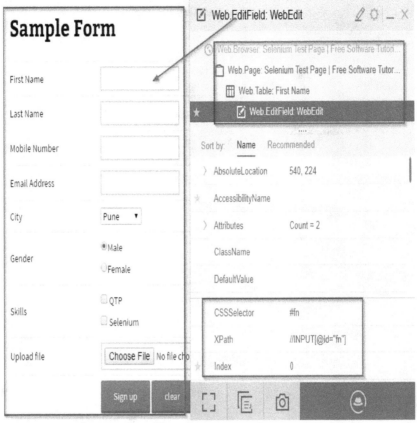

Object Identification Center in LeanFT

5.2 Understanding LeanFT SDK API

Some of the most important packages and classes in LeanFT API are mentioned below.

1. com.hp.lft.report - Reporter class can be used to dump data in report
2. com.hp.lft.sdk - Core functionality
3. com.hp.lft.sdk.insight - used to identify the objects based on images
4. com.hp.lft.sdk.apitesting.uft - UFT API used in LeanFT
5. com.hp.lft.sdk.java - API to automate Java application (Swing/AWT etc)
6. com.hp.lft.sdk.mobile - API to automate mobile applications
7. com.hp.lft.sdk.sap.gui and com.hp.lft.sdk.sap.ui5 - API to automate SAP applications
8. com.hp.lft.sdk.stdwin - API to automate Standard windows applications
9. com.hp.lft.sdk.utils - helper methods
10. com.hp.lft.sdk.web - API to automate Standard Web applications
11. com.hp.lft.sdk.winforms and com.hp.lft.sdk.wpf - API to automate .Net applications
12. com.hp.lft.unittesting and com.hp.lft.unittesting.datadriving - API to work with Unit testing framework of LeanFT
13. com.hp.lft.verifications - It provides Verify class that can be used to assert the expected values

6. New LeanFT project in IntelliJ IDEA

6.1 Installing the LeanFT jar files in Maven Repository

To integrate the LeanFT with Maven, you will have to install the LeanFT library files in local maven repositories.

Execute below commands to install the LeanFT jar files in a local repository.

```
mvn install:install-file -
Dfile="com.hp.lft.sdk-standalone.jar" -
DgroupId="com.hp.lft" -
DartifactId="com.hp.lft.sdk" -
Dversion="12.53.0" -Dpackaging="jar" -
DgeneratePom=true

mvn install:install-file -
Dfile="com.hp.lft.report.jar" -
DgroupId="com.hp.lft" -
DartifactId="com.hp.lft.report" -
Dversion="12.53.0" -Dpackaging="jar" -
DgeneratePom=true

mvn install:install-file -
Dfile="com.hp.lft.unittesting.jar" -
DgroupId="com.hp.lft" -
DartifactId="com.hp.lft.unittesting" -
Dversion="12.53.0" -Dpackaging="jar" -
DgeneratePom=true

mvn install:install-file -
Dfile="com.hp.lft.verifications.jar" -
DgroupId="com.hp.lft" -
DartifactId="com.hp.lft.verifications" -
Dversion="12.53.0" -Dpackaging="jar" -
DgeneratePom=true
```

Then add below dependencies in your POM file.

```xml
            <dependency>
                <groupId>com.hp.lft</groupId>
<artifactId>com.hp.lft.sdk</artifactId>
                <version>12.53.0</version>
            </dependency>

            <dependency>
                <groupId>com.hp.lft</groupId>
<artifactId>com.hp.lft.report</artifactId>
                <version>12.53.0</version>
            </dependency>

            <dependency>
                <groupId>com.hp.lft</groupId>
<artifactId>com.hp.lft.unittesting</artifactId>
                <version>12.53.0</version>
            </dependency>

            <dependency>
                <groupId>com.hp.lft</groupId>
<artifactId>com.hp.lft.verifications</artifactI
d>
                <version>12.53.0</version>
            </dependency>
```

Sometimes you might need to deploy the jar files in organization central repository. Below sample command shows how to deploy LeanFT jar file to central repository.

```
mvn deploy:deploy-file -DgroupId="com.hp.lft" -
DartifactId="com.hp.lft.sdk" -
Dversion="12.53.0" -Dpackaging=jar -
Dfile="com.hp.lft.sdk-standalone.jar" -
DrepositoryId=<id-in-settings.xml> -Durl=<url-
of-the-central-repository>
```

6.2 Creating LeanFT Maven Project

We can create a new LeanFT maven project in IntelliJ IDEA as shown in below images.

Note that once the project is created, you can add required dependencies in POM.xml file.

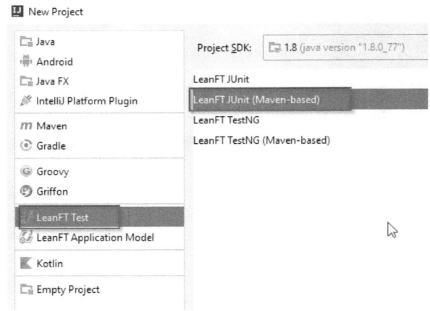

LeanFT Junit Maven project in IntelliJ IDEA

Then enter group id and artifact id for your project and also give the name of the project. Once the maven project is created, add LeanFT dependencies as shown in below image.

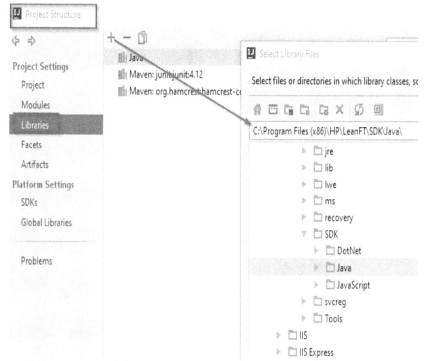

Adding LeanFT libraries to Maven project in IntelliJ IDEA

After that, you can write your tests and enjoy automating applications using LeanFT.

6.3 Creating LeanFT Project with Gradle and TestNG

To create a LeanFT project with Gradle and TestNG, follow below steps.

First of all, create a sample Gradle project in IntelliJ IDEA.

Then add a libs directory under root directory and copy all

LeanFT library files from C:\Program Files (x86)\HP\LeanFT\SDK\Java in it.

Then ensure that your build.gradle file contains below configuration.

```
group 'org.softpost'
version '1.0-SNAPSHOT'

apply plugin: 'java'

repositories {
    mavenCentral()
}

dependencies {
    testCompile group: 'org.testng', name:
'testng', version: '6.9.10'
    compile fileTree(dir: 'libs', include:
'*.jar')
}

test {
    useTestNG {
        suites 'src/test/resources/testng.xml'
    }
}
```

After this, create a sample TestNG test class and add LeanFT test as shown in below example. Notice that you will have to initialize the LeanFT SDK before starting the tests and clean up SDK at the end of tests.

```java
package org.softpost;

import com.hp.lft.report.Reporter;
import org.testng.annotations.AfterClass;
import org.testng.annotations.AfterMethod;
import org.testng.annotations.BeforeClass;
import org.testng.annotations.BeforeMethod;
import org.testng.annotations.Test;

import com.hp.lft.sdk.*;
import com.hp.lft.verifications.*;

import java.net.URI;


public class SimpleLeanFTTest
{

    @BeforeClass
    public void beforeClass()
    {
    }

    @AfterClass
    public void afterClass()
    {
    }

    @BeforeMethod
    public void beforeMethod()
    {
        try
        {
            ModifiableSDKConfiguration config =
new ModifiableSDKConfiguration();
            config.setServerAddress(new
URI("ws://localhost:5095"));
            SDK.init(config);
            Reporter.init();
```

```
        }
        catch (Exception ex)
        {
            System.out.println("Exception
occured " + ex.toString());
        }
    }

    @AfterMethod
    public void afterMethod() throws Exception
    {
        Reporter.generateReport();
        SDK.cleanup();
    }

    @Test
    public void test() throws
GeneralLeanFtException
    {
        Verify.areEqual(22,22,"Verify that 22
== 22");
    }

}
```

After this build your project and then run the tests.

6.4 LeanFT Properties

When we create a LeanFT project using templates, one properties file (leanft.properties) is created and stored in resources directory.

Here are the most important settings in this file that we can use.

1. serverAddress - specify the LeanFT engine address
2. SDK Mode - Replay or Interactive
3. LeanFT Service Address - ws://localhost:5095
4. Connection timeout - 60 sec
5. Response timeout - 600 sec
6. Server autolaunch - true

Here are the most important settings related to LeanFT Report

1. title - Name of the report. By default, it is Run Results.
2. description - Description of the report. By default, it is empty.
3. targetDirectory - Directory where report should be stored. By default it is current directory.
4. overrideExisting - Whether to override existing report. By default, it's value is true.
5. report folder - RunResults
6. override existing - true
7. filter level - All, Warning, Error, Off
8. snapshot level - All, OnError, Off

6.5 Setting up LeanFT project in IntelliJ IDEA

In this topic, we will see how to set up a LeanFT project in IntelliJ IDEA.

We can create a new LeanFT project in 2 ways.

1. Using LeanFT templates
2. Custom framework

If you have installed the LeanFT plugin for IntelliJ IDEA, you can create new project from templates as shown in below image. Note that we can create a project based on 4 types of templates.

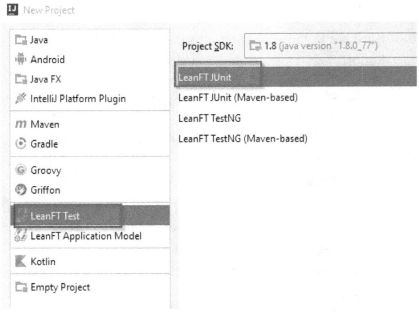

New LeanFT project in IntelliJ IDEA

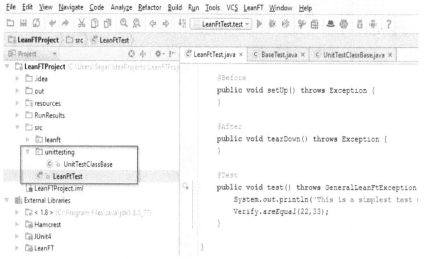

Sample LeanFT project structure

To create your own custom framework, you will have to initialize and clean up SDK as shown in below example. Note that in all upcoming examples, we have inherited BaseTest class.

```
package leanft;

import com.hp.lft.report.Reporter;
import
com.hp.lft.sdk.ModifiableSDKConfiguration;
import com.hp.lft.sdk.SDK;
import org.junit.After;
import org.junit.Before;

import java.net.URI;

public class BaseTest
{
    @Before
    public void test() throws Exception
    {
```

```
        ModifiableSDKConfiguration config = new
ModifiableSDKConfiguration();
        config.setServerAddress(new
URI("ws://localhost:5095"));
        SDK.init(config);
        Reporter.init();
    }

    @After
    public void clean() throws Exception
    {
        Reporter.generateReport();
        SDK.cleanup();
    }
}
```

Then we can write test methods as shown in below
example.

```
package leanft;

import com.hp.lft.report.Reporter;
import com.hp.lft.report.Status;
import
com.hp.lft.sdk.ModifiableSDKConfiguration;
import com.hp.lft.sdk.SDK;
import com.hp.lft.sdk.web.*;
import com.hp.lft.sdk.web.EditField;
import com.hp.lft.sdk.web.EditFieldDescription;
import org.junit.Test;

import java.net.URI;

import static org.junit.Assert.assertEquals;

public class ChromeTest extends BaseTest
{
```

```
@Test
public void test() throws Exception{

    Browser browser =
BrowserFactory.launch(BrowserType.CHROME);
    Try
    {
        //Navigate to
http://www.softpost.org/selenium-test-page/

browser.navigate("http://www.softpost.org/selen
ium-test-page/");
        browser.sync();

    }
    catch(AssertionError ex)
    {
        //Report the Exception

Reporter.reportEvent("Exception","Test failed",
Status.Failed, ex);
        throw ex;
    }
    finally{
        //Close the browser
        browser.close();
    }
  }
}
```

7. LeanFT Project in Eclipse

7.1 Creating maven project with JUnit with LeanFT in Eclipse

Below images will help you understand how to create a maven project with JUnit and LeanFT in Eclipse.

Click on New project menu and then click on Other.

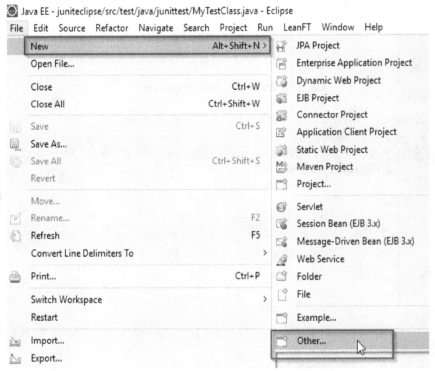

LeanFT - Maven project with JUnit in Eclipse

Then Select LeanFT JUnit Maven project as shown in below image.

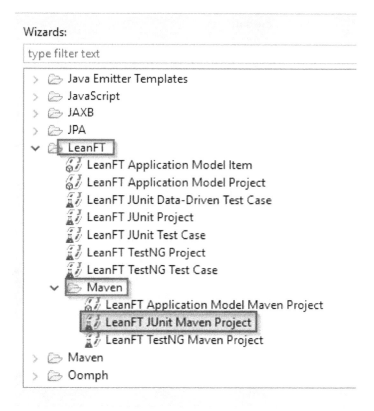

LeanFT - Maven Junit Template in Eclipse

Provide the group id and Artifact id for your project.

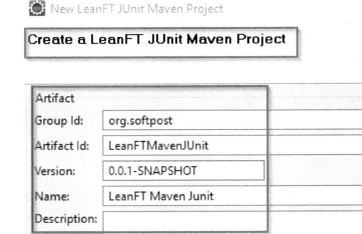

LeanFT - Maven JUnit project in Eclipse

Project is created as shown in below image.

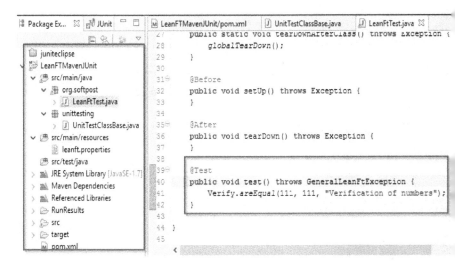

Then add external jars for LeanFT as shown in below image.

Add LeanFT libraries as external jars

After running maven build, you should be able to see the results in RunResults Directory.

7.2 Creating maven project with TestNG in Eclipse

Below images will help you understand how to set up a LeanFT maven project with TestNG in Eclipse.

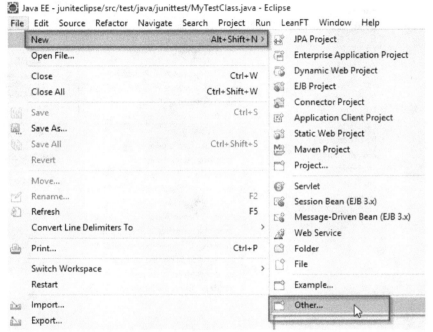

LeanFT - Maven project with JUnit in Eclipse

 New LeanFT TestNG Maven Project

Create a LeanFT TestNG Maven Project

Artifact

Group Id: org.softpost

Artifact Id: testngleanft

Version: 0.0.1-SNAPSHOT

Name:

Description:

Parent Project

Group Id:

Artifact Id:

Version:

LeanFT TestNG group Id in Eclipse

New

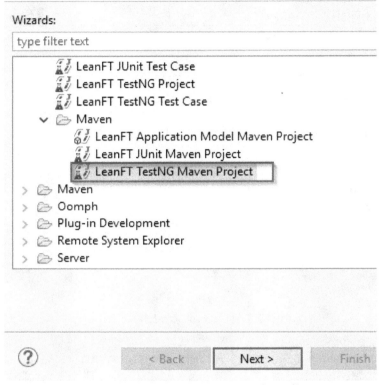

Select a wizard

A Maven project for LeanFT TestNG tests.

Wizards:

type filter text

- LeanFT JUnit Test Case
- LeanFT TestNG Project
- LeanFT TestNG Test Case
- ∨ Maven
  - LeanFT Application Model Maven Project
  - LeanFT JUnit Maven Project
  - LeanFT TestNG Maven Project
- › Maven
- › Oomph
- › Plug-in Development
- › Remote System Explorer
- › Server

(?)   < Back   Next >   Finish

LeanFT TestNG Maven Project in Eclipse

LeanFT puts the tests in src/main/java directory. You should move those test classes to src/test/java because maven always looks in src/text/java directory for any tests to be executed.

8. Object Identification and Management

8.1 Description programming

Usually in UFT, we use object repository (Application model in LeanFT) to store the objects inside application. So we can use those objects in automation code but we can also use description programming to define new test objects in the code itself.

Below example shows how to define new test object using description programming in LeanFT. We have used description programming to define 2 objects of type - EditField and Link. Note that we can multiple property-value pairs to identify the objects.

```java
//Navigate to http://www.softpost.org/selenium-test-page/

browser.navigate("http://www.softpost.org/selenium-test-page/");
    browser.sync();

    //Build edit box object and set value in it

browser.describe(EditField.class,new
EditFieldDescription.Builder()

.id("fn").build()).setValue("Sagar");

    //Build link object and click on it.
            browser.describe(Link.class, new
LinkDescription.Builder()

.tagName("A").innerText("Home").build()).click(
);
```

8.2 Application model

Application models are similar to the object repository in UFT.

We can create a new application model in IntelliJ IDEA as shown in below image.

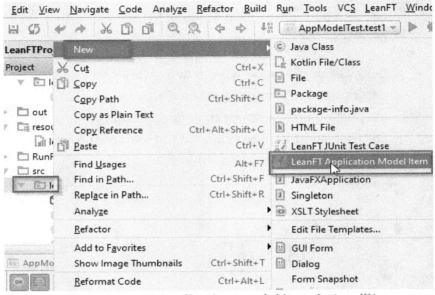

Creating new LeanFT Application model item in IntelliJ IDEA

Below image shows sample AppModel.tsrx file. In designer mode, we can add, remove objects in application model.

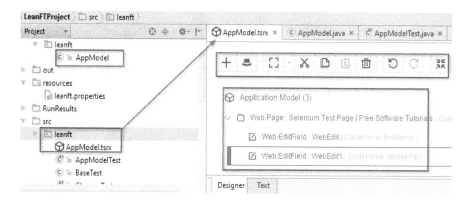

Below image shows how to add the objects to application model using Object Identification Center.

Adding objects in Application model in LeanFT project

Note that 2 files are created after new Application model is created.

1. YourModel.tsrx file -It is an XML file. We can also view this file in design mode where we can add and edit the objects.
2. YourModel.java file containing the code representing the objects in the application model.

Below code shows how to use the application model to write the tests.

```java
package leanft;

import com.hp.lft.sdk.web.Browser;
import com.hp.lft.sdk.web.BrowserFactory;
import com.hp.lft.sdk.web.BrowserType;
import org.junit.Test;

/**
 * Created by Sagar on 22-07-2016.
 */
public class AppModelTest extends BaseTest
{

    @Test
    public void test1() throws Exception
    {
        Browser browser =
BrowserFactory.launch(BrowserType.CHROME);

browser.navigate("http://www.softpost.org/selen
ium-test-page/");
        AppModel model = new AppModel(browser);
```

```
model.SeleniumTestPage().firstName().setValue("
Sagar");
      }
}
```

Another important point to note is that we can use Application model together with description programming to identify the objects as shown in below sample code. Note that we have used SeleniumTestPage object from the Application model but we have used description programming to identify the EditField object inside page.

```
model.SeleniumTestPage().describe(EditField.cla
ss,new EditFieldDescription.Builder()

.id("fn").build()).setValue("Salunke");
```

8.3 Using regular expression in property values

To define the property values of a object, we can use the regular expressions.

Below example shows how to use regular expressions to define the property values. Note that we are clicking on such a link with inner text matching regular expression .*Dev.*

```java
package leanft;
import com.hp.lft.report.Reporter;
import com.hp.lft.report.Status;
import com.hp.lft.sdk.RegExpProperty;
import com.hp.lft.sdk.web.*;
import org.junit.Test;

public class RegularExpressionTest extends
BaseTest
{

    @Test
    public void test() throws Exception
    {

        Browser browser =
BrowserFactory.launch(BrowserType.CHROME);
        Try
        {
            //Navigate to
http://www.softpost.org/selenium-test-page/

browser.navigate("http://www.softpost.org/selen
ium-test-page/");
            browser.sync();

            //set value in edit box

browser.describe(EditField.class,new
EditFieldDescription.Builder()

.id("fn").build()).setValue("Sagar");

    //click on link containing Dev substring
            browser.describe(Link.class, new
LinkDescription.Builder()

.tagName("A").index(1).innerText(new
RegExpProperty(".*Dev.*")).build()).click();
```

```
            //Wait until page loads
            Thread.sleep(3000);
        }
        catch(AssertionError ex)
        {
            //Report the Exception
        Reporter.reportEvent("Exception","Test
failed", Status.Failed, ex);
            throw ex;
        }
        Finally
        {
            //Close the browser
            browser.close();
        }
    }
}
```

We can also use regular expressions to specify values
of object properties in Application Models.

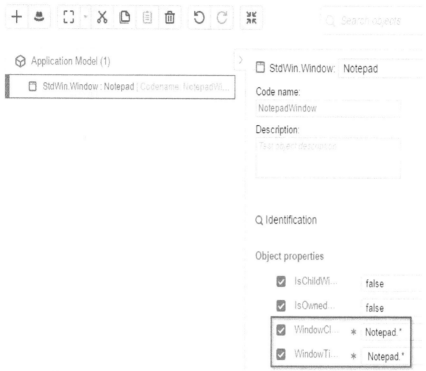

Regular expressions in Application models in LeanFT

9. Automating Web applications

9.1 First web application test

Here is the first web application test using LeanFT. In below code, we are launching the chrome browser and then navigating to http://www.softpost.org/selenium-test-page/. After that we are entering value in edit box and clicking on Home link. Same code will work on other browsers (Firefox, Internet Explorer, Edge) as well. To launch other browsers, you just need to change the browser type in launch method.

```java
package leanft;

import com.hp.lft.report.Reporter;
import com.hp.lft.report.Status;
import com.hp.lft.sdk.ModifiableSDKConfiguration;
import com.hp.lft.sdk.SDK;
import com.hp.lft.sdk.web.*;
import com.hp.lft.sdk.web.EditField;
import com.hp.lft.sdk.web.EditFieldDescription;
import org.junit.Test;

import java.net.URI;

import static org.junit.Assert.assertEquals;

public class ChromeTest extends BaseTest
{
    @Test
    public void test() throws Exception
    {
        Browser browser =
BrowserFactory.launch(BrowserType.CHROME);
```

```
        Try
        {
            //Navigate to
http://www.softpost.org/selenium-test-page/

browser.navigate("http://www.softpost.org/selen
ium-test-page/");
            browser.sync();

            //set value in edit box
   browser.describe(EditField.class,new
EditFieldDescription.Builder()

.id("fn").build()).setValue("Sagar");

            //click on Home link
            browser.describe(Link.class, new
LinkDescription.Builder()

.tagName("A").innerText("Home").build()).click(
);
            //Wait until page loads
            browser.sync();
        }
        catch(AssertionError ex)
        {
            //Report the Exception

Reporter.reportEvent("Exception","Test failed",
Status.Failed, ex);
            throw ex;
        }
        Finally
        {
            //Close the browser
            browser.close();
        }
    }
}
```

Note that BaseTest class provides code to initialize and clean up the LeanFT SDK.

```java
package leanft;

import com.hp.lft.report.Reporter;
import com.hp.lft.sdk.ModifiableSDKConfiguration;
import com.hp.lft.sdk.SDK;
import org.junit.After;
import org.junit.Before;
import java.net.URI;

public class BaseTest
{
    @Before
    public void init()
    {
        try
        {
            ModifiableSDKConfiguration config = new ModifiableSDKConfiguration();
            config.setServerAddress(new URI("ws://localhost:5095"));
            SDK.init(config);
            Reporter.init();
        }
        catch (Exception ex)
        {
            System.out.println("Exception occured " + ex.toString());
        }
    }
    @After
    public void clean() throws Exception
    {
        Reporter.generateReport();
        SDK.cleanup();
    }
}
```

9.2 Identifying the Web elements using XPATH and CSS

We can use XPATH and CSS selectors to identify the web elements. Below example illustrates how to use XPATH and CSS in LeanFT.

In below example, we have identified edit box using XPATH and CSS.

For more advanced XPATH expressions, you can visit - http://selenium-interview-questions.blogspot.in/2014/02/how-to-identify-elements-using-xpath-in.html

For more advanced CSS expressions, you can visit - http://selenium-interview-questions.blogspot.in/2014/02/how-to-identify-elements-using.html

```
package leanft;

import com.hp.lft.report.Reporter;
import com.hp.lft.report.Status;
import com.hp.lft.sdk.web.*;
import org.junit.Test;

public class CssXpathTest extends BaseTest
{
    @Test
    public void test() throws Exception
    {
        Browser browser =
BrowserFactory.launch(BrowserType.CHROME);
        Try
        {
```

```
              //Navigate to
http://www.softpost.org/selenium-test-page/

browser.navigate("http://www.softpost.org/selen
ium-test-page/");
            browser.sync();

            //set value in edit box using xpath

browser.describe(EditField.class,new
EditFieldDescription.Builder()

.xpath("//input[@id='fn']").build()).setValue("
Sagar");

            //set value in edit box using css

browser.describe(EditField.class,new
EditFieldDescription.Builder()

.cssSelector("input[id='fn']").build()).setValu
e("Salunke");

        }
        catch(AssertionError ex)
        {
            //Report the Exception

Reporter.reportEvent("Exception","Test failed",
Status.Failed, ex);
            throw ex;
        }
        Finally
        {
            //Close the browser
            browser.close();
        }
    }
}
```

9.3 Identifying objects using Visual Relational Identifiers – VRI

This is the advanced feature in UFT and LeanFT that allows you to identify the objects based upon the position of adjacent objects. For example in below image we can identify the edit box using text associated with it.

Selenium Test Page

This is a sample selenium test page.

Sample Form

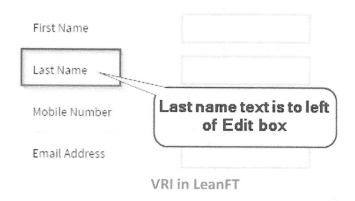

VRI in LeanFT

Here is the complete example that shows how to use VRI in LeanFT. Note that we can provide multiple visual relational identifiers to identify a object.

```java
package leanft;
import com.hp.lft.report.Reporter;
import com.hp.lft.report.Status;
import com.hp.lft.sdk.HorizontalVisualRelation;
import com.hp.lft.sdk.VisualRelation;
import com.hp.lft.sdk.web.*;
import org.junit.Test;

public class VriTest extends BaseTest
{
    @Test
    public void test() throws Exception
    {
        Browser browser =
BrowserFactory.launch(BrowserType.CHROME);
        Try
        {
            //Navigate to
http://www.softpost.org/selenium-test-page/

browser.navigate("http://www.softpost.org/selen
ium-test-page/");
            browser.sync();

            //set value in edit box

browser.describe(EditField.class,new
EditFieldDescription.Builder()

.id("fn").build()).setValue("Sagar");

    WebElement e2 =
browser.describe(WebElement.class,new
WebElementDescription.Builder()
    .xpath("//td[text()='Last
Name']").build());

browser.describe(EditField.class,new
EditFieldDescription.Builder()
```

```
                    .vri(new
VisualRelation().setTestObject(e2).

setHorizontalRelation(HorizontalVisualRelation.
LEFT_AND_INLINE)).build())
                    .setValue("Salunke");

        //click on Home link
        browser.describe(Link.class, new
LinkDescription.Builder()

.tagName("A").innerText("Home").build()).click(
);

            //Wait until page loads
            browser.sync();
        }
        catch(AssertionError ex)
        {
            //Report the Exception

Reporter.reportEvent("Exception","Test failed",
Status.Failed, ex);
            throw ex;
        }
        Finally
        {
            //Close the browser
            browser.close();
        }
    }
}
```

9.4 Handling embedded browser control in Windows app

Sometimes, Windows application have elements that embed the browser control. To identify the elements inside the browser control as Web elements, you will have to register the browser control with LeanFT.

To register the browser control with LeanFT, follow below steps.

1. Launch the utility - C:\Program Files (x86)\HP\LeanFT\bin\SettingNewBrowserControlApplication.exe

2. Then enter the path of the application that contains browser control in the utility window and click on register

3. Finally you need to restart the LeanFT engine.

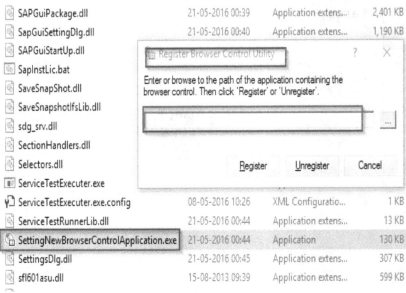

Registering browser control with LeanFT

Once the browser control is registered, all objects inside it will be identified as web objects.

Note that LeanFT can handle browser control based on IE engine only!

9.5 Firing events on Web Elements using LeanFT

We can fire html events like click, change etc on any Web element using EventInfo class in LeanFT.

Here is the complete example that illustrates how to fire events.

```java
package leanft;

import com.hp.lft.report.Reporter;
import com.hp.lft.report.Status;
import com.hp.lft.sdk.NativeObject;
import com.hp.lft.sdk.web.*;
import org.junit.Test;

import java.util.List;

public class ChromeNativeObjectTest extends BaseTest
{
    @Test
    public void test() throws Exception
    {
        Browser browser =
BrowserFactory.launch(BrowserType.CHROME);
        try{
            //Navigate to
http://www.softpost.org/selenium-test-page/

browser.navigate("http://www.softpost.org/selen
ium-test-page/");
```

```
                browser.sync();

                //set value in edit box

browser.describe(EditField.class,new
EditFieldDescription.Builder()

.id("fn").build()).setValue("Sagar");

        browser.describe(Link.class, new
LinkDescription.Builder()

.tagName("A").innerText("Home").build()).fireEv
ent(EventInfoFactory.createEventInfo("click"));
                Thread.sleep(3000);

        }
        catch(AssertionError ex)
        {
            //Report the Exception

Reporter.reportEvent("Exception","Test failed",
Status.Failed, ex);
            throw ex;
        }
        Finally
        {
            //Close the browser
            browser.close();
        }
    }
}
```

Alternatively, you can also execute custom JavaScript using below syntax.

```
String html =
browser.getPage().runJavaScript("document.body.
innerHTML;");
```

To fire change event on element with id -fn, You can use below Javascript as argument to runJavaScript() method.

```
var evt = document.createEvent('HTMLEvents');
evt.initEvent ('change', true, true);
document.findElementById('fn').dispatchEvent(ev
t);
```

9.6 Executing JavaScript in web page

While automating web applications, you might need to execute the JavaScript to perform certain operations.

LeanFT allows you to execute custom JavaScript as shown in below example. We can use runJavaScript method of Page class to execute any valid JavaScript.

```java
package leanft;

import com.hp.lft.report.Reporter;
import com.hp.lft.report.Status;
import com.hp.lft.sdk.web.*;
import com.hp.lft.verifications.Verify;
import org.junit.Test;

public class ExecuteJavaScriptTest extends
BaseTest
{
    @Test
    public void test() throws Exception
    {

        Browser browser =
BrowserFactory.launch(BrowserType.INTERNET_EXPL
ORER);
        Try
        {
            //Navigate to
http://www.softpost.org/selenium-test-page/

browser.navigate("http://www.softpost.org/selen
ium-test-page/");
            browser.sync();
            String html =
browser.getPage().runJavaScript("document.body.
innerHTML;");
```

```
            System.out.println("HTML Source of
the page" + html);
            System.out.println("Scrolling to
120,100");

browser.getPage().runJavaScript("window.scrollT
o(120,100);");

            String documentState =
browser.getPage().runJavaScript("document.ready
State");
            System.out.println("Document State
is " + documentState);

        }
        catch(AssertionError ex)
        {
            //Report the Exception

Reporter.reportEvent("Exception","Test failed",
Status.Failed, ex);
            throw ex;
        }
        Finally
        {
            //Close the browser
            browser.close();
        }
    }
}
```

10. Automating windows applications

10.1 Automating standard windows application

To automate the standard windows apps, you will need to import below packages in LeanFT project.

com.hp.lft.sdk.stdwin

Here is the sample application that launches the notepad and enters text in it. Then it tries to close the notepad. After that it clicks on Don't save button on the Dialog box.

```java
package leanft;

import com.hp.lft.sdk.Desktop;
import com.hp.lft.sdk.stdwin.*;
import org.junit.Test;

import static org.junit.Assert.assertEquals;

public class NotepadTest extends BaseTest
{
    @Test
    public  void test() throws Exception
    {
        new
ProcessBuilder("C:\\Windows\\System32\\notepad.exe").start();

        Thread.sleep(3000);

        Window notepadWin =
Desktop.describe(Window.class,
                new
WindowDescription.Builder().windowTitleRegExp("Notepad").build());
```

```
        Editor editor =
notepadWin.describe(Editor.class,
                new
EditorDescription.Builder().nativeClass("Edit")
.windowClassRegExp("Edit").build());

        editor.sendKeys("This is automated
text");

        Thread.sleep(3000);
        notepadWin.close();

        Desktop.describe(Window.class, new
WindowDescription.Builder()

.ownedWindow(false).childWindow(false).windowCl
assRegExp("Notepad").windowTitleRegExp("
Notepad").build())
                .describe(Dialog.class, new
DialogDescription.Builder()

.ownedWindow(true).childWindow(false).text("Not
epad").nativeClass("#32770").build())
                .describe(Button.class, new
ButtonDescription.Builder()
                .text("Do&n't
Save").nativeClass("Button").build()).click();
    }
}
```

10.2 Automating Java Application

Automating the Java applications is just like that of Standard windows applications. Only difference is that you need to import classes in below package.

import com.hp.lft.sdk.java.*;

Here is the sample example that identifies the Java window with title - XYZ and then clicks on the check box with attached text as "Gender" inside a frame.

```java
package leanft;

import com.hp.lft.sdk.CheckedState;
import com.hp.lft.sdk.Desktop;
import com.hp.lft.sdk.java.*;
import org.junit.Test;

public class JavaTest extends BaseTest
{

    @Test
    public void test() throws Exception
    {
        Window javaWin =
Desktop.describe(Window.class, new
WindowDescription.Builder()
                .title("XYZ").build());

        CheckBox checkBox =
javaWin.describe(InternalFrame.class, new
InternalFrameDescription.Builder()

.title("Frame1").build()).describe(CheckBox.cla
ss, new CheckBoxDescription.Builder()

.attachedText("Gender").build());
```

```
checkBox.setState(CheckedState.CHECKED);
    }
}
```

10.3 Automating WPF applications

Below example illustrates how to automate WPF application using LeanFT. Note that we need to import classes from below package.

com.hp.lft.sdk.wpf

In below example, we are first identifying the WPF window with title - Bus Application. After that we have identified the ComboBox with name sourceCity and finally we have listed down all the options in sourceCity ComboBox.

```
package leanft;

import com.hp.lft.sdk.Desktop;
import com.hp.lft.sdk.wpf.ComboBox;
import com.hp.lft.sdk.wpf.ComboBoxDescription;
import com.hp.lft.sdk.wpf.Window;
import com.hp.lft.sdk.wpf.WindowDescription;
import org.junit.Test;

/**
 * Created by Sagar on 20-07-2016.
 */
public class WpfTest extends BaseTest
  {
    @Test
    public void test1() throws Exception
      {
```

```
        Window win =
Desktop.describe(Window.class, new
WindowDescription.Builder()
                .objectName("Bus
Application").fullType("window").windowTitleReg
Exp("Bus Application").build());

        ComboBox box=
win.describe(ComboBox.class, new
ComboBoxDescription.Builder()

.objectName("sourceCity").build());

        for (String s :box.getItems())
        {
            System.out.println(s);
        }

    }
}
```

10.4 Automating SAP Application

Automating SAP applications is very much similar to automation of standard windows applications.

Please note that you will have to use classes from below SAP packages.

```
import com.hp.lft.sdk.sap.gui.*;
import com.hp.lft.sdk.sap.ui5.*;
```

11. Synchronization

By default, LeanFT will wait for 20 seconds when trying to find the objects. If it doesn't identify the object withing 20 seconds, exception is thrown.

You can change this timeout from LeanFT settings dialog.

Additionally you can also add custom wait conditions.

```java
package leanft;

import com.hp.lft.sdk.GeneralLeanFtException;
import com.hp.lft.sdk.*;
import com.hp.lft.sdk.stdwin.ToolBar;
import com.hp.lft.sdk.stdwin.Window;
import com.hp.lft.sdk.stdwin.WindowDescription;
import org.junit.Assert;
import org.junit.Test;

/**
 * Created by Sagar on 21-07-2016.
 */
public class SynchTest extends BaseTest
{
    @Test
    public void test1() throws Exception
    {

WaitUntilTestObjectState.WaitUntilEvaluator<Win
dow> evaluator = new
WaitUntilTestObjectState.WaitUntilEvaluator<Win
dow>() {
            @Override
            public boolean evaluate(Window
testObject) throws GeneralLeanFtException
            {
```

```
                return
testObject.getWindowState()==WindowState.MAXIMI
ZED;
            }
        };
        new
ProcessBuilder("C:\\Windows\\System32\\notepad.
exe").start();

        Window notepadWindow =
Desktop.describe(Window.class,
                new
WindowDescription.Builder().windowClassRegExp("
Notepad").windowTitleRegExp("Notepad").build())
;
        notepadWindow.maximize();

Assert.assertTrue(evaluator.evaluate(notepadWin
dow));
    }
}
```

12. Assertions and Reports

12.1 Assertions in LeanFT

We can do assertions in LeanFT using Verify class in Validations namespace.

This class allows you to put the assertions in the code. Here is the sample example showing usage of Verify class.

Note that Verify class provides below methods.

1. areEqual , areNotEqual
2. isTrue, isFalse
3. startsWith, contains, endsWith
4. lessOrEqual, less, greater, greaterOrEqual
5. isMatch
6. isNullOrEmpty, isNotNullOrEmpty

```java
package leanft;

import com.hp.lft.report.Reporter;
import com.hp.lft.report.Status;
import com.hp.lft.sdk.ModifiableSDKConfiguration;
import com.hp.lft.sdk.SDK;
import com.hp.lft.sdk.web.*;
import com.hp.lft.sdk.web.EditField;
import com.hp.lft.sdk.web.EditFieldDescription;
import com.hp.lft.verifications.Verify;
import org.junit.Test;
import java.net.URI;
import static org.junit.Assert.assertEquals;

public class ChromeTest extends BaseTest
{
    @Test
```

```
    public void test() throws Exception
    {
        Browser browser =
BrowserFactory.launch(BrowserType.CHROME);
        Try
        {
            //Navigate to
http://www.softpost.org/selenium-test-page/

browser.navigate("http://www.softpost.org/selen
ium-test-page/");
            browser.sync();

            //set value in edit box

browser.describe(EditField.class,new
EditFieldDescription.Builder()

.id("fn").build()).setValue("Sagar");

            //click on Home link
            browser.describe(Link.class, new
LinkDescription.Builder()

.tagName("A").innerText("Home").build()).click(
);
            //Wait until page loads
            browser.sync();

Verify.isTrue(browser.getTitle().toLowerCase().
contains("tutorial"),"Verifying the title of
Home page");

        }
        catch(AssertionError ex)
        {
            //Report the Exception

Reporter.reportEvent("Exception","Test failed",
Status.Failed, ex);
```

```
            throw ex;
        }
        Finally
        {
            //Close the browser
            browser.close();
        }
    }
}
```

Here is the HTML report showing verification point.

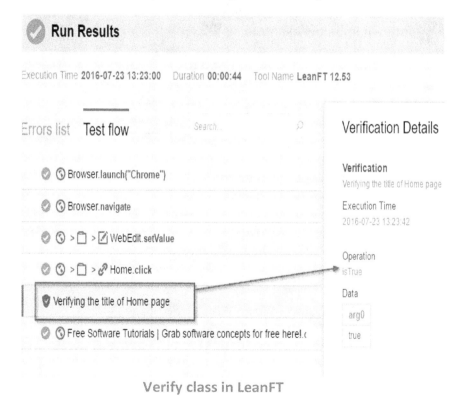

Verify class in LeanFT

12.2 Generating reports with screenshots and recordings

Reports can be generated in 2 ways in LeanFT.

1. Screenshots using Reporter and TestObject.GetSnapshot
2. Video recordings of test execution using Microsoft expression encoder.

By default, LeanFT creates the reports in RunResults folder in the root directory of Java project. But you can change that using ModifiableReportConfiguration class as shown in below example.

You can also use below method to send your log messages to the report.
Reporter.reportEvent

```java
package leanft;

import com.hp.lft.report.*;
import com.hp.lft.sdk.Desktop;
import com.hp.lft.sdk.stdwin.Window;
import com.hp.lft.sdk.stdwin.WindowDescription;
import com.hp.lft.sdk.web.*;
import com.hp.lft.verifications.Verify;
import org.junit.Test;

import java.awt.image.RenderedImage;

public class ChromeReportTest extends BaseTest
{
    @Test
    public void test() throws Exception
    {
```

```java
        ModifiableReportConfiguration
reportConfig =
ReportConfigurationFactory.createDefaultReportC
onfiguration();
        reportConfig.setOverrideExisting(true);

reportConfig.setTargetDirectory("RunResults");
// The folder must exist under C:\

reportConfig.setReportFolder("myreportdirectory
");
        reportConfig.setTitle("My Report
Title");
        reportConfig.setDescription("Report
Description");

reportConfig.setSnapshotsLevel(CaptureLevel.OnE
rror);
        Reporter.init(reportConfig);
        Browser browser =
BrowserFactory.launch(BrowserType.CHROME);

        Try
        {
            //Navigate to
http://www.softpost.org/selenium-test-page/

browser.navigate("http://www.softpost.org/selen
ium-test-page/");
            browser.sync();

            //set value in edit box
            EditField firstName =
browser.describe(EditField.class,new
EditFieldDescription.Builder()
            .id("fn").build());
            firstName.setValue("Sagar");

            //take screenshot
```

```
            RenderedImage img =
browser.getPage().getSnapshot();

            if
(firstName.getValue().equalsIgnoreCase("sagar")
)
                Reporter.reportEvent("Verify
Editbox","Value is sagar", Status.Passed,img);
            else
                Reporter.reportEvent("Verify
Editbox","Value is not sagar",
Status.Failed,img);

        }
        catch(AssertionError ex)
        {
            //Report the Exception

Reporter.reportEvent("Exception","Test failed",
Status.Failed, ex);
            throw ex;
        }
        Finally
        {
            //Close the browser
            browser.close();
        }
    }
}
```

Here is the sample report generated by above code.

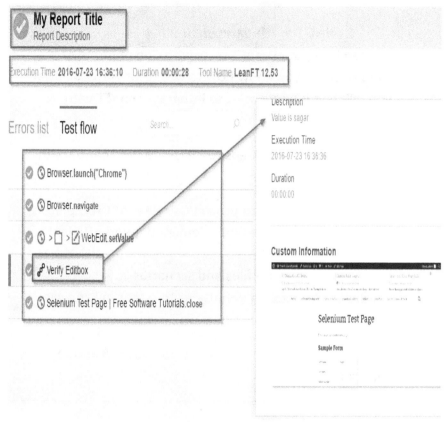

HTML report in LeanFT showing screenshot captured during run

13. LeanFT Frameworks

13.1 LeanFT with Cucumber

We can integrate LeanFT tests with Cucumber BDD framework. If you know how to use JUnit with Cucumber, you will find it very easier to integrate LeanFT with Cucumber.

Please follow below steps to integrate the LeanFT with Cucumber.

1. Create a maven project using LeanFT template
2. Add cucumber and selenium dependency in POM.xml
3. Write feature files and scenarios
4. Write the step definitions for steps in Scenario
5. Execute feature file

Here is the dependency that you will have to add for cucumber.

```xml
<dependency>
    <groupId>info.cukes</groupId>
    <artifactId>cucumber-java</artifactId>
    <version>1.2.4</version>
    <scope>test</scope>
</dependency>
```

Then you have to create a feature file as shown in below example.

```
Feature: My feature

  Scenario: My Scenario
    Given I am on www.softpost.org page
    Then I verify that title contains tutorial
word
```

After that you can create step definitions as shown in below example.

```java
package org.softpost;

import com.hp.lft.report.Reporter;
import
com.hp.lft.sdk.ModifiableSDKConfiguration;
import com.hp.lft.sdk.SDK;
import com.hp.lft.sdk.web.Browser;
import com.hp.lft.sdk.web.BrowserFactory;
import com.hp.lft.sdk.web.BrowserType;
import cucumber.api.java.After;
import cucumber.api.java.Before;
import cucumber.api.java.en.Given;
import cucumber.api.java.en.Then;
import org.junit.Assert;

import java.net.URI;

/**
 * Created by Sagar on 23-07-2016.
 */
public class Steps
{
    Browser browser;
    @Before
    public void init() throws Exception
```

```java
    {
        ModifiableSDKConfiguration config = new
ModifiableSDKConfiguration();
        config.setServerAddress(new
URI("ws://localhost:5095"));
        SDK.init(config);
        Reporter.init();
    }

    @Given("^I am on www\\.softpost\\.org
page$")
    public void i_am_on_www_softpost_org_page()
throws Throwable
    {
        browser =
BrowserFactory.launch(BrowserType.CHROME);

browser.navigate("http://www.softpost.org");
    }

    @Then("^I verify that title contains
tutorial word$")
    public void
i_verify_that_title_contains_tutorial_word()
throws Throwable
    {

Assert.assertTrue(browser.getTitle().toLowerCas
e().contains("tutorial"));
    }

    @After
    public void clean() throws Exception
    {
        browser.close();
        SDK.cleanup();
    }
}
```

13.2 Keyword Driven frameworks

Keyword driven frameworks are very popular in LeanFT.

Please follow below steps to create keyword driven framework.

1. Find main operations and features of the application.
2. Map each feature or operation to a keyword.
3. Write a code to automate specific keyword.
4. Create test sheet containing test cases made up of one or more keywords. You can store the test sheet in Excel file, Database or in the form of JUnit or TestNG test class.
5. Unless you are using JUnit or TestNG to execute the tests, you might need to create a driver script to execute each test case.

Here is the case study on WPF Flight application provided by HP.

In this application, we can create a keyword for each major feature like log in to the application, searching a flight, selecting a flight, Placing a order, Searching a order, Deleting the order, Cancelling the order, Book a flight, Verify flights.

Then we can create test cases for various user scenarios using same keywords as mentioned above.

Here are couple of test cases created using above keywords. Note that in below test cases, we have re-used login keyword.

Here is the test case to search for a flight.

1. Login to the Flight application.
2. Search for the flights from London to Paris in next week for one person.
3. Verify that flights are displayed from London to Paris only.

Here is the test case to search for a order.

1. Login to the Flight application.
2. Book a flight and note down order number say 88.
3. Search for order with id 88.
4. Verify that flight details are correctly displayed.

13.3 Data Driven Frameworks

Data driven framework are used when you need to test the application with various types of data.

You can store the data in below formats.

1. Microsoft Excel Files
2. Databases

In data driven frameworks, we test the same feature but with different set of data. For example, in HP flight application, we can test the Login functionality with various combination of User Id and Password.

Note that here Login functionality is same but Test data is different during each run.

14. Converting the UFT Object Repository to Application models in LeanFT

We can use below command line utility to convert the Object repository to Application models in LeanFT.

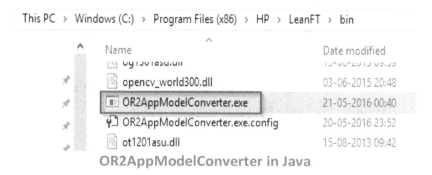

This PC > Windows (C:) > Program Files (x86) > HP > LeanFT > bin

	Name	Date modified
	~~ug1301asu.dll~~	~~15-06-2015 05:55~~
📌	opencv_world300.dll	03-06-2015 20:48
📌	OR2AppModelConverter.exe	21-05-2016 00:40
📌	OR2AppModelConverter.exe.config	20-05-2016 23:52
📌	ot1201asu.dll	15-08-2013 09:42

OR2AppModelConverter in Java

Here is the syntax of this utility.

OR2AppModelConverter myuftOR.tsr myAppModel.tsrx myLogFile.log Warning

First argument is the path of the object repository file. Second argument is the path of the application model file. Third argument is the path of the log file and last argument is the log level (It can be Info, Warning or Error).

15. Integrating the LeanFT tests with CI servers

15.1 Adding maven task in Bamboo

The important settings of maven task are given below.

1. Provide the path of maven executable
2. Provide any valid maven goal

Below image shows how to configure the maven task in Bamboo. We have set up the clean test goal.

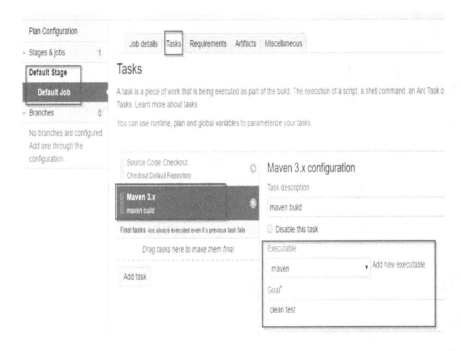

maven task in Bamboo

Below image shows the sample output of the build plan using maven task.

```
build   11-Jun-2016 11:55:17    [INFO]
build   11-Jun-2016 11:55:17    [INFO] --- maven-compiler-plugin:3.1:compile (default-compile) @ testng-artifact ---
build   11-Jun-2016 11:55:21    [INFO] Changes detected - recompiling the module!
build   11-Jun-2016 11:55:21    [INFO] Compiling 1 source file to C:\Users\Sagar\Downloads\atlassian-bamboo-5.12.1\bin\UsersSagarbam
build   11-Jun-2016 11:55:26    [INFO]
build   11-Jun-2016 11:55:26    [INFO] --- maven-resources-plugin:2.6:testResources (default-testResources) @ testng-artifact ---
build   11-Jun-2016 11:55:26    [INFO] Using 'UTF-8' encoding to copy filtered resources.
build   11-Jun-2016 11:55:26    [INFO] Copying 1 resource
build   11-Jun-2016 11:55:27    [INFO]
build   11-Jun-2016 11:55:27    [INFO] --- maven-compiler-plugin:3.1:testCompile (default-testCompile) @ testng-artifact ---
build   11-Jun-2016 11:55:27    [INFO] Changes detected - recompiling the module!
build   11-Jun-2016 11:55:27    [INFO] Compiling 1 source file to C:\Users\Sagar\Downloads\atlassian-bamboo-5.12.1\bin\UsersSagarbam
classes
build   11-Jun-2016 11:55:27    [INFO]
build   11-Jun-2016 11:55:27    [INFO] --- maven-surefire-plugin:2.19.1:test (default-test) @ testng-artifact ---
build   11-Jun-2016 11:55:29
build   11-Jun-2016 11:55:29    -------------------------------------------------------
build   11-Jun-2016 11:55:29     T E S T S
build   11-Jun-2016 11:55:29    -------------------------------------------------------
build   11-Jun-2016 11:55:30    Running TestSuite
build   11-Jun-2016 11:55:31    ...
build   11-Jun-2016 11:55:31    ... TestNG 6.9.10 by Cédric Beust (cedric@beust.com)
build   11-Jun-2016 11:55:31    ...
build   11-Jun-2016 11:55:31
build   11-Jun-2016 11:55:32    Test1
build   11-Jun-2016 11:55:32    PATH=C:\Program Files\Java\jdk1.8.0_77\bin;C:\ProgramData\Oracle\Java\javapath;C:\Program Files
(x86)\Lenovo\FusionEngine;C:\WINDOWS\system32;C:\WINDOWS;C:\WINDOWS\System32\Wbem;C:\WINDOWS\System32\WindowsPowerShell\v1.0\;C:\Pro
Files\lenovo\easyplussdk\bin;C:\Program Files (x86)\ATI Technologies\ATI.ACE\Core-Static;C:\Program Files (x86)\QuickTime\QTSystem\;
Files\Git\bin;C:\Users\Sagar\AppData\Local\Android\sdk\platform-tools;C:\PROGRA~2\Groovy\GROOVY~1.6\bin;C:\Program Files (x86)\Windo
Live\Shared;C:\WINDOWS\system32\config\systemprofile\.dnx\bin;C:\Program Files\Microsoft DNX\Dnvm\;C:\Program Files\Microsoft SQL
Server\130\Tools\Binn\;C:\Windows\Microsoft.NET\Framework64\v4.0.30319;C:\Program Files (x86)\Microsoft Visual Studio 14.0\Common7\I
2.13\bin;C:\Program Files\Java\jdk1.8.0_77\bin;C:\maven\apache-maven-3.3.9\bin;C:\Windows\Microsoft.NET\Framework64\v4.0.30319;C:\Pr
14.0\Common7\IDE;C:\Users\Sagar\Downloads\gradle-2.13-bin\gradle-2.13\bin
build   11-Jun-2016 11:55:32    BAMBOO_BUILDKEY=MP-TES-JOB1
build   11-Jun-2016 11:55:32    MAVEN2_HOME=C:\maven\apache-maven-3.3.9
build   11-Jun-2016 11:55:32    _RUNJAVA="C:\Program Files\Java\jdk1.8.0_77\jre\bin\java.exe"
build   11-Jun-2016 11:55:32    BAMBOO_CAPABILITY_SYSTEM_BUILDER_MSBUILD_MSBUILD_V2_0__32BIT_=C:\WINDOWS\Microsoft.NET\Framework\v2.
build   11-Jun-2016 11:55:32    SESSIONNAME=Console
build   11-Jun-2016 11:55:32    ALLUSERSPROFILE=C:\ProgramData
```

maven output in Bamboo

15.2 Creating and Configuring the builds in Jenkins

Now let us understand how to create and configure a typical build in Jenkins.

To create new build (also called as job), click on New Item link on Jenkins Home page. It will open below page.

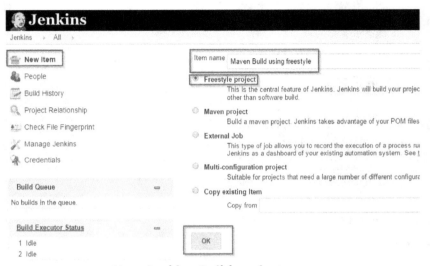

New Jenkins Build project

Then enter name of project, select freestyle project option and click on OK. It will open Build configuration page as shown below. Enter project description and add parameter if you want pass any parameter to the build.

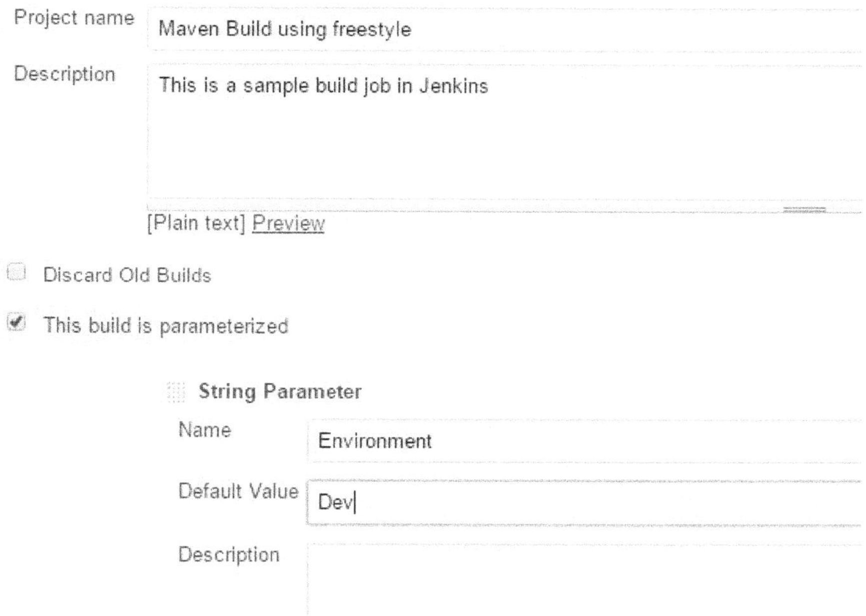

Project name
Maven Build using freestyle

Description
This is a sample build job in Jenkins

[Plain text] Preview

☐ Discard Old Builds

☑ This build is parameterized

String Parameter

Name
Environment

Default Value
Dev|

Description

Build configuration in Jenkins - Build name, description, parameters

Next you need to configure the SCM like git as shown in below image. In this example, we are using repository on GITHUB. But you can use any other version control software.

git - Source code management in Jenkins build

Next - you have to specify the build triggers. You can specify the trigger in the form of Cron expressions. You can also poll SCM at regular intervals and if changes are detected, build will be run.

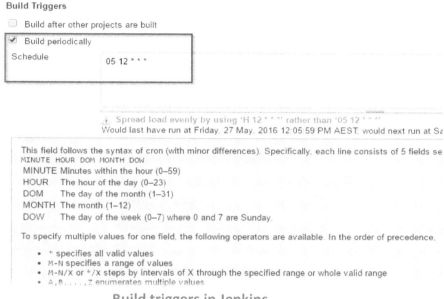

Build triggers in Jenkins

Your job/project is made up of multiple build steps. So you can add build steps as shown in below image. Note that you will not see all build steps as shown in below image unless you have installed proper plugins. For examples - MSBuild step will not be available unless you install MSBuild plugin in Jenkins.

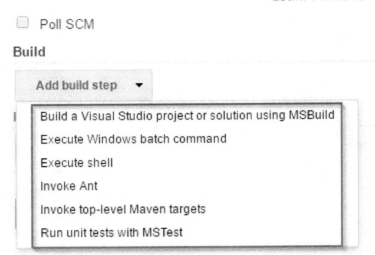

Build steps in Jenkins

maven build step in Jenkins

Last thing you need to do is configure post-build actions. Below image shows possible post-build actions that you can do.

post-build actions in Jenkins

Above step is optional. So just go ahead and click on Save button. Well done! You have just created a sample build in Jenkins. To view your build project, just go to homepage. You will see your build(Highlighted in yellow color) as shown in below image.

S	W	Name	Last Success	Last Failure	Last Duration	
		Complex Build	N/A	N/A	N/A	
		Maven Build	1 mo 24 days - #91	1 hr 47 min - #106	16 min	
		Maven Build using freestyle	N/A	4 min 11 sec - #2	57 sec	
		Shell Build	54 min - #1	N/A	3 sec	
		Visual Studio Build	N/A	1 hr 47 min - #1	2.5 sec	
		Windows Batch Build	59 min - #2	N/A	1.7 sec	

All +

Icon: S M L

Legend RSS for all RSS for failures RSS for just latest builds

Jenkins build on Dashboard

15.3 Build steps for Maven project in TeamCity

In this topic, you will learn how to set up a build steps for maven project in TeamCity.

As shown in below image, you have to select runner type as Maven. Then you have to provide the goals to be executed. By default, it uses POM.xml in the root directory of the project. You may also run code coverage process along with test goal which gives report on how many classes were covered by tests.

Here is the list of some of the popular maven goals that can be used.

1. test - execute tests using surefire plugin. We can also pass various parameters to maven JUnit test goal and maven testNG test goal
2. verify - executes unit tests as well as does verification provided by plugins
3. install
4. site
5. deploy

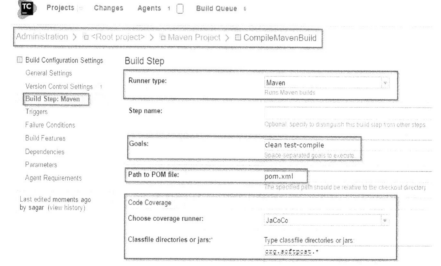

maven build step in TeamCity

Below image shows that sample build log.

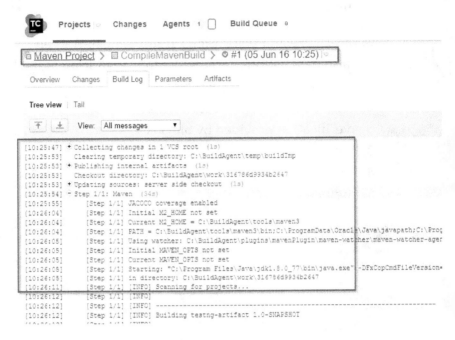

maven build log in TeamCity

16. Challenges and Solutions

16.1 Challenges of LeanFT automation

Here is the list of main LeanFT challenges.

1. LeanFT does not support third party controls. We have to use Native objects to automate such third party objects.
2. Dynamic Elements like check boxes, buttons, radio buttons inside nested tables. We have to use HTML DOM to handle such elements.

16.2 Working with third party objects using

Native Object properties and methods

Below example illustrates how to access native object properties in LeanFT. In below example, we have set the value in edit box using native value property. We have also used native click method to click on Home link.

```java
package leanft;

import com.hp.lft.report.Reporter;
import com.hp.lft.report.Status;
import com.hp.lft.sdk.NativeObject;
import com.hp.lft.sdk.web.*;
import org.junit.Test;

import java.util.List;

public class ChromeNativeObjectTest extends
BaseTest
{
```

```java
@Test
public void test() throws Exception{

    Browser browser =
BrowserFactory.launch(BrowserType.CHROME);
    Try
    {
        //Navigate to
http://www.softpost.org/selenium-test-page/

browser.navigate("http://www.softpost.org/selen
ium-test-page/");
        browser.sync();

        //set value in edit box

browser.describe(EditField.class,new
EditFieldDescription.Builder()

.id("fn").build()).setValue("Sagar");


        //get native object
        NativeObject obj =
browser.describe(EditField.class,new
EditFieldDescription.Builder()

.id("fn").build()).getNativeObject();

        //list native members of the object
        List<String> list =
obj.getMembers();

        for (String  s : list  )
        {
            System.out.println(s);
        }

        obj.setProperty("value","Native");
```

```
            Thread.sleep(3000);

        //click on Home link using native
click method
            browser.describe(Link.class, new
LinkDescription.Builder()

.tagName("A").innerText("Home").build()).getNat
iveObject().invokeMethod("click");
        }
        catch(AssertionError ex)
        {
            //Report the Exception

Reporter.reportEvent("Exception","Test failed",
Status.Failed, ex);
            throw ex;
        }
        Finally
        {
            //Close the browser
            browser.close();
        }
    }
}
```

17. LeanFT common issues and solutions

I have listed down common issues and solutions that you may encounter while working with LeanFT.

1. Failed to connect to LeanFT run time engine on....This exception comes when LeanFT run time engine is not running. Just start the engine and this error should vanish.

2. An Internal problem has occurred, please make sure the LeanFT SDK was properly initialized....This exception comes when you have not initialized LeanFT SDK. To get rid of this exception, add below lines at the beginning of the code.

```
ModifiableSDKConfiguration config = new
ModifiableSDKConfiguration();

config.setServerAddress(new
URI("ws://localhost:5095"));

SDK.init(config);
```

3. IntelliJ IDEA does not start when LeanFT is plugin is enabled – To fix this issue kill the LeanFT plugin for IntelliJ IDEA in process explorer

4. com.hp.lft.sdk.ReplayObjectNotUniqueException: Object not unique – This exception comes when LeanFT finds more than one object matching the description. To fix this issue, you need to add more properties so that only one object is identified.

5. Object not found – This exception comes when LeanFT is not able to find the object in the application. To fix this issue, ensure that object really exists in the application and you are using correct description to identify the object.

18. Comparing LeanFT with other tools

18.1 Difference between HP UFT and LeanFT

Here is the list of main differences between UFT and LeanFT.

1. UFT scripts can be written in VBScript only.
2. LeanFT scripts can be written in languages like Java, C#.Net and Java script.
3. LeanFT does not support automation of various technologies like Oracle, Siebel, PeopleSoft, Delphi, Power Builder, Stingray, Flex, VisualAge. UFT supports all these platforms.

18.2 Comparison of LeanFT with Selenium and Ranorex

Based upon my experience, I can say that LeanFT and Ranorex are equivalent in terms of features.

Difference between Selenium and LeanFT

1. Biggest difference between Selenium and LeanFT (and Ranorex) is that Selenium can only support automation of web pages and not windows applications. But LeanFT and Ranorex can automate the windows and forms very easily along with web application.
2. Another major difference between Selenium and other 2 tools is that Selenium is free!

Difference between LeanFT and Ranorex

1. LeanFT is developed by HP while Ranorex is developed by Ranorex Gmbh.
2. Ranorex coding can be done only in C#.Net While LeanFT can be coded in C#.Net as well as Java.
3. Ranorex uses xpath to identify objects in windows as well as web applications. LeanFT uses property value pairs to identify the objects in Windows apps. LeanFT also supports xpath in web applications.

19. LeanFT Java References

You can find the LeanFT resources at below urls.

1. http://leanft-help.saas.hpe.com/en/12.52/HelpCenter/Content/HelpCenterRoot/DemoApps.htm - Demo applications provided by HP

2. http://leanft-help.saas.hpe.com/en/12.52/JavaSDKReference/index.html?com/hp/lft/sdk/example-files/master-examples-list.html - Sample examples in Java

3. http://leanft-help.saas.hpe.com/en/12.52/JavaSDKReference/index.html - LeanFT Java SDK

4. http://leanft-help.saas.hpe.com/en/12.52/HelpCenter/Content/HowTo/UFT_OR_Converter.htm - Coverting UFT Object repository into Application models in LeanFT

5. http://leanft-help.saas.hpe.com/en/12.52/HelpCenter/Content/HowTo/RunRemotely.htm - Executing the tests remotely in LeanFT

6. http://leanft-help.saas.hpe.com/en/12.52/HelpCenter/Content/HowTo/CI_Tools.htm - Integrating LeanFT with CI servers like TeamCity

www.ingramcontent.com/pod-product-compliance
Lightning Source LLC
Chambersburg PA
CBHW060942050326
40689CB00012B/2554